THE STORY OF
STANLEY AND STEVEN

By BLAKE HOENA

Illustrated by DOREEN MULRYAN

Music Arranged and Produced by STEVEN C MUSIC

CANTATA
LEARNING

WWW.CANTATALEARNING.COM

CANTATA
LEARNING

Published by Cantata Learning
1710 Roe Crest Drive
North Mankato, MN 56003
www.cantatalearning.com

A note to educators and librarians from the publisher: Cantata Learning has provided the following data to assist in book processing and suggested use of Cantata Learning product.

Publisher's Cataloging-in-Publication Data
Prepared by Librarian Consultant: Ann-Marie Begnaud
Library of Congress Control Number: 2015958208
    The Story of Stanley and Steven
    Series: Read, Sing, Learn : Sound It Out!
    By Blake Hoena
    Illustrated by Doreen Mulryan
    Summary: A song about the st letter blend.
    ISBN: 978-1-63290-611-3 (library binding/CD)
    ISBN: 978-1-63290-651-9 (paperback/CD)
Suggested Dewey and Subject Headings:
    Dewey: E FIC
    LCSH Subject Headings: Brothers – Juvenile humor. | Brothers – Songs and music – Texts. | Brothers – Juvenile sound recordings.
    Sears Subject Headings: Brothers. | Phonetics. | School songbooks. | Children's songs. | Popular music.
    BISAC Subject Headings: JUVENILE FICTION / Family / Siblings. | JUVENILE FICTION / Stories in Verse. | JUVENILE FICTION / Humorous Stories.

Book design and art direction, Tim Palin Creative
Editorial direction, Flat Sole Studio
Music direction, Elizabeth Draper
Music arranged and produced by Steven C Music

Printed in the United States of America in North Mankato, Minnesota.
072016   0335CGF16

Take the letter S. Now add a T. These two letters blend together to make the ST sound. The ST sound usually comes at the beginning or the end of a word. Thanks to this sound, you can *st*and and *st*omp. You can come in fir*st* when you run fa*st*.

Ready to *st*art? Turn the page and let's sing!

Now, come hear the story of Stanley and his brother.
Oh, Stanley had a brother and his name was Steven.

Come hear the story of Stanley's little brother.
Oh, Stanley's favorite thing was to bug poor Steven.

While Stanley stared at Steven,
he would make big bug eyes.
He'd stare at him and stomp around
and stick out his tongue.

While Stanley stood and stared,
   he made the biggest bug eyes.
He'd stare and stomp around
   until Steven had enough!

Then Steven would yell,
"Stop. Stop it. Stop it!"

"It? Stop It? Stop what?"
Stanley had to ask.

"Oh, what is this great, mysterious It?
How do I stop It, and what does It do?"

Steven just sat there, all still as he **stewed**,
and Stanley laughed as he sang out of tune.

"Oh, what is this great, mysterious It?
A beast that stings or a monster that stomps?

Or is It a **stout** stegosaurus
with **steely** horns that will poke us?"

Steven just sat there, all still as he stewed,
and Stanley laughed as he sang out of tune.

Stick around, and hear Steven's side of our story.
Oh, he did some stuff to bug his big brother, too.

Won't you stay and hear Steven's side of our story?
He did **stealthy** stuff like sneaking into Stanley's room.

Steven stepped up on a stool
    and started to stir things up.
He'd stick socks here
    and stow toys there,
    moving Stanley's stuff.

Steven stood up on a stool
and messed up Stanley's things.
He'd stack stuff everywhere
until his brother had enough!

PUZZLE

Then Stanley would yell,
"Stop. Stop it. Stop it!"

"It? Stop It? Stop what?"
Steven had to ask.

"Oh, what is this great, mysterious It?
How do I stop It, and what does It do?"

Stanley just sat there, all still as he stewed,
and Steven laughed as he sang out of tune.

PUZZLE

19

"Oh, what is this great, mysterious It?
A beast that stings or a monster that stomps?

Or is It a stout stegosaurus
with steely horns that will poke us?"

They both just sat there, all still as they stewed.
Then the brothers laughed and sang out of tune.

SONG LYRICS
The Story of Stanley and Steven

Now, come hear the story of Stanley and his brother.
Oh, Stanley had a brother and his name was Steven.

Come hear the story of Stanley's little brother.
Oh, Stanley's favorite thing was to bug poor Steven.

While Stanley stared at Steven, he would make big
    bug eyes.
He'd stare at him and stomp around and stick out
    his tongue.

While Stanley stood and stared, he made the biggest
    bug eyes.
He'd stare and stomp around until Steven had enough!

Then Steven would yell, "Stop. Stop it. Stop it!"
"It? Stop It? Stop what?" Stanley had to ask.

"Oh, what is this great, mysterious It?
How do I stop It, and what does It do?"
Steven just sat there, all still as he stewed,
and Stanley laughed as he sang out of tune.

"Oh, what is this great, mysterious It?
A beast that stings or a monster that stomps?
Or is It a stout stegosaurus
with steely horns that will poke us?"

Steven just sat there, all still as he stewed,
and Stanley laughed as he sang out of tune.

Stick around, and hear Steven's side of our story.
Oh, he did some stuff to bug his big brother, too.

Won't you stay and hear Steven's side of our story?
He did stealthy stuff like sneaking into Stanley's room.

Steven stepped up on a stool and started to stir things up.
He'd stick socks here and stow toys there, moving
    Stanley's stuff.

Steven stood up on a stool and messed up Stanley's things.
He'd stack stuff everywhere until his brother had enough!

Then Stanley would yell, "Stop. Stop it. Stop it!"
"It? Stop It? Stop what?" Steven had to ask.

"Oh, what is this great, mysterious It?
How do I stop It, and what does It do?"
Stanley just sat there, all still as he stewed,
and Steven laughed as he sang out of tune.

"Oh, what is this great, mysterious It?
A beast that stings or a monster that stomps?
Or is It a stout stegosaurus
with steely horns that will poke us?"

They both just sat there, all still as they stewed.
Then the brothers laughed and sang out of tune.

The Story of Stanley and Steven

Pop
Steven C Music

Verse

1. Now, come hear the sto-ry of Stan-ley and his broth-er. Oh, Stan-ley had a broth-er and his name was Ste-ven. Come hear the sto-ry of

Stan-ley's lit-tle broth-er. Oh, Stan-ley's fav-or-ite thing was to bug poor Ste-ven. Then

Verse 2
While Stanley stared at Steven, he would make big bug eyes.
He'd stare at him and stomp around and stick out his tongue.
While Stanley stood and stared, he made the biggest bug eyes.
He'd stare and stomp around until Steven had enough!

Pre Chorus

Ste-ven would yell, "Stop. Stop it. Stop it!" "It? Stop It? Stop what?" Stan-ley had to ask.
(Stan-ley)   (Ste-ven)

Chorus

a Tempo
"Oh, what is this great, mys-te-ri-ous It? How do I stop It, and what does It do?"

Ste-ven just sat there, all still as he stewed, and Stan-ley laughed as he sang out of tune.
(Stan-ley)   (Ste-ven)

"Oh, what is this great, mys-te-ri-ous It? A beast that stings or a mon-ster that stomps? Or is It a stout steg-o-saur-us with stee-ly horns that will

poke us?" Ste-ven just sat there, all still as he stewed, and Stan-ley laughed as he sang out of tune.
(Stan-ley)   (Ste-ven)

Verse 3
Stick around, and hear Steven's side of our story.
Oh, he did some stuff to bug his big brother, too.
Won't you stay and hear Steven's side of our story?
He did stealthy stuff like sneaking into Stanley's room.

Verse 4
Steven stepped up on a stool and started to stir things up.
He'd stick socks here and stow toys there, moving Stanley's stuff.
Steven stood up on a stool and messed up Stanley's things.
He'd stack stuff everywhere until his brother had enough!

Pre Chorus

Chorus

Coda

They both just sat there, all still as they stewed. Then the broth-ers laughed and sang out of tune.

23

GLOSSARY

stealthy—quiet and sneaky

steely—made of steel

stewed—stayed mad

stout—short and wide

GUIDED READING ACTIVITIES

1. On pages 13 and 20, Stanley and Steven sing about different monsters. Draw how you imagine these monsters would look.

2. Looking at the pictures in the story, how many things can you find that start with ST?

3. Make a list of words that have the ST sound, such as star, stomach, storm, beast, and feast. How many words can you come up with?

TO LEARN MORE

Houran, Lori Haskins. *Flat Stanley and the Very Big Cookie*. New York: Harper, 2015.

Manushkin, Fran. *Big Sisters Are the Best*. Mankato, MN: Picture Window Books, 2012.

Wegwerth, A. L. *Stegosaurus*. Mankato, MN: Capstone Press, 2015.

Weiss, Ellen, and Mel Friedman. *The Stinky Giant*. New York: Random House Children's Books, 2012.